REVERSED THUNDER

REVERSED THUNDER
NOTES ON SOME CONTEMPORARY CATHOLIC POETS

GREGORY STEPHENSON

Ober-Limbo Verlag

Grateful acknowledgement is made to the editors
of the publications in which these pieces first
appeared: *Catholic Books Review, Eclectica, Empty
Mirror* and *Midwest Book Review*.

Published by Ober-Limbo Verlag
Heidelberg, Germany

ISBN 978-87-971569-4-0

Cover photo, design & layout: Birgit Stephenson

For Birgit
Involuntary Genius

CONTENTS

From the Root of Light:
Elizabeth Jennings / page 9

The Soul in Paraphrase:
Paul Quenon / page 17

The View from the Moon:
John Slater / page 23

At the Borders of Being:
Sally Read / page 31

What Will Suffice:
The Nuns of Mariakloster / page 39

Prayer the church's banquet, angel's age,
God's breath in man returning to his birth,
The soul in paraphrase, heart in pilgrimage,
The Christian plummet sounding heav'n and
   earth
Engine against th' Almighty, sinner's tow'r,
Reversed thunder ...

Prayer (I)
   George Herbert

FROM THE ROOT OF LIGHT

By powerful opposing forces within her own mind and spirit, Elizabeth Jennings (1926-2001) was alternately laid waste and raised again, torn and made whole. Her life bears all the stigmata of a contemporary *poète maudit:* poverty, mental illness, unrequited love, suicide attempts, institutionalization, alcoholism, loneliness. At the same time, she was also a deeply dedicated, proficient and prolific, award-winning poet, honoured in 1992 by Queen Elizabeth II with an O.B.E. (Commander of the Order of the British Empire.) Jennings was also a devout – if sometimes conflicted – Roman Catholic, of decidedly mystical inclination. Her work remains under-appreciated and in America largely unknown.

New Selected Poems brings together 166 poems gleaned by the author and the editor, Rebecca Watts, from 21 volumes of Jennings' poems, written over six decades (from 1953 to 2001.) The poems are for the most part short lyrics cast in traditional forms, though later in her career Jennings wrote occasionally in free verse. Unlike many of her fellow poets in the postwar period, Jennings found writing in regular metre and end-rhyme not a constriction of her imagination but a liberation. Within the formal pattern of rhythm and rhyme she works with great technical skill, but her poems are far from tidy and kempt; beneath their elegance and ingenuity they are informed by rending tensions and dark energies. Each poem is thus a kind of temporary victory of order and hope over despair and disorder.

Seeking communion with life in the wider world, Elizabeth Jennings writes of fishermen and children, teenagers riding a bus and the tender love of old couples, of nuns and nurses, love affairs and the deaths of friends, of patients in a mental hospital and a lonely little boy, of mountaineers, statues, a diamond-cutter and a still-born child, of flies and thunder, beech leaves and grapes, stars, trees, birds, flowers, the moon, the seasons, and of paintings and painters: Chagall, Bonnard, Rembrandt, Andrea Mantegna, Samuel Palmer and David Jones. There are descriptive poems and devotional poems, elegies and meditations, poems of personal memory and self-scrutiny, poems portraying moments of naked despair and moments of illumination.

While each of Jennings' poems is distinct and autonomous, informed by its own means and ends, the individual poems can most fully be understood, I think, as interlinked expressions of a central underlying theme of perception, by which I mean the way in which reality is apprehended by human eyes and minds. In close relation to this bedrock theme, there is a theme of spiritual conflict and growth in the life of the poet-speaker.

The theme of perception is evident already in Jennings' earliest poems, such as "Reminiscence," where the poet contrasts the sensual unpatterned apprehension of the world she possessed as a child with her present overly subtle and confused consciousness. Similarly, in "The Idler," the poet-speaker acknowledges the wisdom of a disparaged social outsider in seeing and appreciating what is immediately before his senses, rather than wishing to accelerate or striving to anticipate its future state. In observing a rose, the idler does not, Jennings writes, "colour it with his own shadow, as we contrive, living beyond the present, / To move all things away from their present moment."

Jennings deepens and broadens the theme of perception through many subsequent poems, writing in "In this Time" that as a culture we have – to our loss and our peril – severed ourselves from the profound truths of myth and legend and have "retreated inwards to our minds / ... have made rooms there with all doors closed, / All windows shuttered." In "Beyond Possession," she writes of the way in which as adults we no longer perceive the things of the world – a rose, a river – as they are but only according to the images we project upon them through habit and egocentricity. "All is itself," she states, but we have rendered ourselves incapable of perceiving things as themselves, in themselves and for themselves, seeing them instead exclusively in terms of ourselves, each separate sundered human individual interpreting the external world in terms of "a mind reflecting his own face."

"Thunder and a Boy" depicts the divergent responses to a thunder storm made by "us" (acculturated, habituated adults) and by a boy watching the lightning by night from a window. We have forgotten or dismissed, Jennings asserts, the wonder once elicited in our spirits by such an event. In naming (and explaining) the elements of heaven we have sought to deny their primal power and to subjugate them, to assert over them ourselves, our power. In contrast to our predetermined, reductive response to the naked beauty and raw force of a thunder storm, the boy feels exalted and moved to awe. In "Beginning," the poet-speaker recalls a similar – gentler yet more intense, epiphanic – occurrence from her early childhood:

"I stood at a window once. I was four or five
And I watched the sun open the garden and spread out
the grass
And I heard the far choir of some blackbirds and watched
blue flowers rise.
This was the first day for me, the planet alive,
And I watched the stars' shadows grow faint and finally pass
And I could not believe my eyes. "

Other aspects of the theme of perception are treated in a number of other poems by Jennings but an equal number of her poems describe the sense of desolation, the discord and division, the brokenness and confusion experienced by the poet-speaker when clarity of perception and reciprocal connectivity with the world are lost, overwhelmed from within by darkness and disorder. In "To a Friend with a Religious Vocation," the first-person speaker expresses distress at the implacable power of an invasive force inhabiting her mind: "the dark, the dark that draws me back / Into a chaos where / Vocations, visions fail, the will grows slack / And I am stunned by silence everywhere." There follow several harrowing poems written by Jennings in a mental hospital, including "Night Garden of the Asylum," conveying in potent compression the infernal estrangement from the world as experienced by her and her fellow sufferers in their affliction:

"The all is broken from its fullness.
A human cry cuts across a dream.
A wild hand squeezes an open rose.
We are in witchcraft, bedevilled. "

After poems of collapse and disconnection, there come poems of recovery and reconnection to the natural world and to deep currents of the spirit. Even following her release from the hospital, the poet remains acutely aware of "The terrible depth / of dark in me" ("A Litany for Contrition.) Beech leaves clinging to winter branches, bare winter grape vines, the hatching of a bird's egg, a hand embroidery, a frail-seeming but firm tree are all embraced by her as emblems and omens of endurance and perseverance. There continue to be hard hours for the poet-speaker, hours "when hope seems as far as the furthest star," but once again she achieves moments of joy, regaining a sense of God as immanent in the visible world. More than ever, the writing of poetry is seen by Jennings as a sacred act, a spell against the darkness within, for, as she affirms, poetry rises "from the root of light" ("Against the Dark.") And, as expressed in the poem "Is it Dual Natured?" her convalescence summons in her a brave resolve to live and strive according to her own sense of truth: "I will risk all extremes, I will flounder, will stumble, will burn."

In Elizabeth Jennings' study of "mystical experience and the making of poems," *Every Changing Shape* (London: Andre Deutsch, 1961) the author remarks that "the poems which satisfy most are not those which simply give a sense of reconciliation and order, but those which show life and order as the fruits of conflict." (108) The poems of Jennings' last years are distinguished by this latter quality. The praise and celebration of the visible world and of the invisible Presence within and beyond it

which informs these late poems has the feeling of a grace
gained through harrowing dispossession.

In "Into the Hour," the poet speaks with humility of "the
hour of a white healing ... a sudden sunlit hour" when the wide
wound of inward loss is lost and the world is seen as a singing.
Deploying similar imagery of light and music, "The Way of
Words and Language" counsels those who may have lost their
way in life that their dark night will ultimately end and there
will be "a time of silence and light like a shielded lamp" when
"you are found and safe at last." Attaining this blessed state of
spirit, the spirit will then be transfigured into song.

"Star Gazing" gives form again to the theme of perception,
linking it to a spiritual optics, arguing that by imposing onto
natural phenomena designs and definitions of our own
construction we become blind to their mystery and meaning.
The eye must be unsealed, the mind disimprisoned to see the
true luminous and numinous nature of things. The stars in the
night sky, she argues, are not to be possessed by our presump-
tuous petrified formulae, they must be *seen,* received in wonder,
beheld with the perceptual innocence of childhood: "The sky is
pouring silver rain." Another poem of night and stars and
spiritual optics, Jennings' last poem of all, "Assurance Beyond
Midnight," tells of "clarities" that come in the solitude of the
small hours, affirmations of faith, when there is contact with
"everything that's peace," and the conviction that in the end all

things work for the best. "Sickness and heartbreaks" and all that is sombre notwithstanding, seen with a dark-adapted eye, the world we inhabit is, after all, "a golden world."

A woman and a Catholic, Elizabeth Jennings was not altogether at home in the mainstream of English postwar poetry, neither among the traditionalists nor the modernists. Her affinities were with other Christian visionary poets, such as Thomas Traherne (1636-1674) and Gerard Manley Hopkins (1844-1889) with whom she shared a view of natural beauty as a reflection of divine Presence. Jennings' well-wrought poems are at once modest and honest, stripped of inessentials, yet bold and rich, possessing a freshness and a strangeness that seize our attention, sustain our interest and ultimately secure our admiration. In theme and form, she went her own way as a poet, following the contours of her own experience, according to the intelligence of her heart. Her poetry offers us many bright gifts, many genuine and precious things.

New Selected Poems by Elizabeth Jennings
Edited by Rebecca Watts
Manchester: Carcanet Press, 2019

THE SOUL IN PARAPHRASE, HEART IN PILGRIMAGE

The coincidence of a vocation as monk and a vocation as poet –
though far from commonplace – is one that occurs often
enough so as not to be entirely unfamiliar to many readers of
poetry. There are, for example, the celebrated monk-poets of
the East: Han Shan and Shide, Chia Tao and Ching An of China;
Ryokan and Tonna, Shikei and Sogi of Japan; while in the
Western tradition, there are the anonymous Irish monk-poets
of the middle ages, Caedmon and John Lydgate in England,
Gonzalo de Berceo and Luis de Léon in Spain, and in our own
era, the English Benedictine monk and concrete poet Dom
Sylvester Houédard, and the American monk-poet Thomas
Merton. These are but a few names among many others. The
overlap between the two vocations through time and across
cultural lines might be attributable to their shared requisites of
openness and attention, together with an inclination possessed
in common to understand things (such as the ultimate nature
of reality) in relational terms, that is to say through figurative
language.

Paul Quenon is a Trappist monk and a poet. *Amounting
to Nothing* is the seventh and most recent collection of his
poems, following upon *Unquiet Vigil: New and Selected Poems,*

published in 2014. (1) The letters "OSCO" appended to his name,
signify that he is a member of the Order of Cistercians of the
Strict Observance, a Roman Catholic contemplative religious
order whose lives are dedicated to seeking union with God.
Quenon came to the order as a novice in 1958 at the age of
seventeen, and is a member of the monastic community at the
Abbey of Gethsemeni in rural Kentucky. As Brother Quenon
relates in his acclaimed memoir, *In Praise of the Useless Life* –
and as may be inferred from his poems which often celebrate
the natural world – for prayer and meditation he prefers to sit
outdoors, and, indeed, year round in all weathers prefers to
sleep outdoors in a sleeping bag. (2) He is at present nearly 80
years old.

Spare and clear, written with wit and precision, Quenon's
poems keep close to the elemental, to the essentials of expe-
rience. His poems are cast both in regular metre and end-rhyme
and in various forms and shapes of free verse. The topics range
from fireflies and spiders to deer and coyotes, racoons and
crickets, mockingbirds and juncos, trees and flowers, stars and
seasons, weathers and clouds, fellow monks and kitchen
utensils, tractors and "the fine art of frying an egg." There are
descriptive and reflective poems, devotional poems, odes and
elegies, and poems inspired by memories and dreams. A deep
engagement with nature informs his writing. Recurrent themes
include time, mortality and reality. But despite their serious

concerns, several poems here are touched with mischievous humor, including puns, parody and paradox.

The sly wordplay at work in the volume's title, is echoed in the first poem in the collection, titled "Mad Monk's Life Ambition." With self-deflating humor the poet-speaker of the verse laments his failure in not having amounted to *nothing*. To have stripped himself of received habits of thought and feeling, to have erased altogether every self-serving impulse of the shallow surface self (thereby amounting to *nothing*) was his goal as a monk. While recognizing that at present he does not "amount to a hill of beans," he still aspires ultimately to amount to "a hill of humus," that is to say the dark, organic material that forms when plant and animal matter (the ego self) decays. Out of such fertile soil might come, he hopes, new life, out of the humus left by the breakdown of the false, external self might emerge a deeper, truer self.

A poem whose subject and underlying theme linger long afterward to puzzle the mind of the reader is "Critical Change for Whom?" Quenon depicts here a conversation he is having with a friend and fellow monk in which the friend questions the reality of the material world, contending that it is all an illusion. "Reality," his friend maintains, "is other." Quenon is reluctant to enter into argument with his friend, but – indicating the individual furnishings of the room in which their discussion is taking place – states that he is himself inclined to "take what I see for what it is." Inwardly, Quenon worries that his friend is oppressed by such "dark concerns" and is "in for a critical change." At this point of the poem, the scene changes abruptly and completely. Quenon has awakened from what was a dream of speaking with his friend about the nature of reality. It is night and Quenon is alone, sleeping outdoors under the stars. His friend is three years dead. The friend's words as spoken in the dream – " the dream he knew was a dream" – take on a powerful resonance. The world Quenon now beholds has been knocked atilt.

Another poem, titled "A Song," comprises a baffling, koan-like question and response:

> What slips between the in
> and the out of my breath?
> What does the mountain
> always know?
>
> The ground, the ground,
> the ground only,
> and more, the ground.

A haunting riddle. The answer is as enigmatic as the question. But the mystery that informs both riddle and reply invites the reader's intuitive mind to engage with it. Perhaps in doing so we may gain purchase on an elusive truth, one concerning the relation between the ground on which we live and move and to which ultimately we return, and the Ground of Being.

Metaphors and similes are scant among the poems in this volume, but Quenon makes recurrent use of anthropomorphization, ascribing human attributes to non-human entities and natural phenomena. The creatures, objects and events he endows with consciousness and emotions in his poems include trees, thunder, the sun and moon, clouds, birds, wind, snow, flowers, grass, planets, cold and heat, rain, dogs, dawn and geese, racoons and coyotes. This poetic practice on the part of Quenon derives, I believe, from a sacramental apprehension of the world, a conviction that all created things are sustained in their existence by God, and that God is substantially present in every aspect and particular of the created world. There is, the poems imply, a numinous mystery at the heart of things, a sacred interconnectedness among all terrestrial beings and processes. Far from turning away from the world – as many people mistakenly believe that monks do – Brother Quenon turns toward the world, approaching it with humility, observing it with a loving wonder and a reverent attention, finding lessons among insects, discovering instruction in blossoms and in a robin's song, and reading revelations in clouds.

In these crisp, well-crafted poems are to be found depth and strength, clarity and grace, quiet beauty and a gentle, subtle

wisdom. In the deepest meaning of prayer – to address God
with adoration or thanksgiving – Brother Quenon's poems may
be seen to comprise prayers. In ways beyond formal orisons and
beyond our ordinary linguistic resources these poems articulate
such prayer as the poet-priest George Herbert (1593-1633)
termed "the soul in paraphrase, heart in pilgrimage." (3)

NOTES
1. *Unquiet Vigil: New and Selected Poems* by Paul Quenon,
    Brewster, Massachusetts: Paraclete Press, 2014.
2. *In Praise of the Useless Life: A Monk's Memoir* by Paul
    Quenon, Notre Dame, Indiana: Ave Maria Press, 2018.
3. *"Prayer (I)"* by George Herbert, *The Poetical Works of
    George Herbert,* New York: D. Appleton & Co., 1857, p. 61.

Amounting to Nothing
by Paul Quenon, OSCO
Brewster, Massachusetts:
Paraclete Press, 2019

THE VIEW FROM THE MOON

John Slater is the nom-de-plume of Father Isaac Slater, a
Trappist monk at The Abbey of the Genesee, located
near Piffard, in Livingston County, New York. He has to
date published two collections of his poetry: *Surpassing
Pleasure* (2011) and *Lean* (2019.) Slater's poems – cast in
traditional forms and free verse – are skillful and fluent, and
immediately engaging. Each of his poems has something to say
and usually says it with intensity and grace, and not infre-
quently with subtle touches of humor, as reflected in the
punning titles of a number of the poems gathered in *Surpassing
Pleasure.*

Apart from imbuing the poems with a mildly mischievous
spirit, the punning also serves, I think, to suggest curious
connections between disparate concepts or phenomena: waves
and waving, hips and hipness, moving belongings and being
moved, varieties of "the snowball effect," divergent senses of
"having what it takes," "falling asleep," "building on sand," and
more.

The same fine pitch of feeling and observation that
permits Slater to perceive unexpected valences among common

words and idioms also informs his often oblique perspectives on
things, "the view from the moon," as he phrases it in the poem
"Floodgate." There are, the poet reminds us, other ways of
seeing and understanding, alternative approaches to the
phenomenal world from which unaccustomed inferences may
be drawn.

Itching and scratching, for example, may ultimately be
seen to be a metaphysical issue, an Alcoholics Anonymous
meeting may be looked upon as a sanctified occasion, a snooker
champion may be an advanced Zen practitioner, microscopic
parasites may play a giant role in maintaining the planet, the
shabby outcast cadging drinks from monks during a Holy Week
celebration may be no less a celebrant than his hosts, a family's
markedly differing styles of swimming may be secretly syn-
chronized, a man's anger may be camouflaging his anguish,
chess games, soccer matches and even arguments may in reality
represent forms of quest "for the depths of contemplation,"
("Homo Ludens") instructions for the assembly of optical
instruments may sometimes profitably be dispensed with, the
Dewey Decimal system in use in libraries might with advantage
be replaced by a new method of cataloguing books "based on
Blake, each section / with appropriate body part or mythic
character, a vision map / of suburban sprawl, a subdivided
jigsaw puzzle of watered lawns." ("Revising the Book of Urizen.")

Our lives on this earth are seen by Slater as situated "between eternal fields of light." ("Making Waves.") In the interim we are tasked with discerning and holding to the *Real* (as the theologian John Hick has named it.) That is to say: the good, the true, the holy, that which is of ultimate value. Far from being censorious or sanctimonious, though, Slater is humbly and sympathetically aware of how difficult such an endeavor is for us all, how many pitfalls beset our several paths through this world, how easily we may be waylaid or ambushed or go astray, how many lives are painful, lonely, hindered and stunted. He is also well aware of the very real presence of an intractable, wily and conniving "Mr. Hyde" resident in the psychic basement of each of us. ("Snowball Effect.")

In the discipline of a trained skin diver, in the resignation of a sand sculptor, in the gravity-defying skills of a master carpenter, in the honed poems of an ancient Chinese hermit poet, in the focused chess moves of an ex-con, in the witty self-accusations of an anonymous medieval scribe, in the egoless magnanimity of a saint, in the patient, practiced compassion of an aged monk, Slater finds inspiring exemplars of meticulous attention, models of self-mastery. And, drawing upon his own experience working as a gardener, Slater also takes spiritual encouragement from the ingenuity of bees, from the brave endurance of a frail azalea and the resilience of pruned trees, and from the sheer dedication of bamboo. The attentive,

receptive gardener, Slater affirms, will learn "not to make order
from chaos or / impose the design of his own will but / grow
each plant shrub pine or flowering fruit tree according to its
impulse / to underline its native leanings." ("Grounded.") Such
assent to the bent of things might be seen as another way of
saying "Thy will be done."

Slater writes in a casual, companionable voice but each
word is placed with care, each phrase weighed and set to
measure, each simile and allusion well-fitted to the motif of the
poem. Flexible in their styles and varied in form and theme,
pivoting gracefully from whimsy to reverence, from matter to
metaphysics, his poems are – in every sense – spirited. There is
a truth at the center of his work, something genuine and
profound.

The poems in Slater's second collection, *Lean,* are – as the
title of the volume suggests – spare. They are rigorously com-
pressed and tersely worded, with narrow lines (from one to four
words in length.) Their rhythms are angular, their imagery stark
and their similes few. These are poems whetted to a fine edge.

The first stanza of the first poem in *Lean* describes with
concision the process by which irritants such as "grit, sand, /
bits of debris" provoke in shell-bearing molluscs the formation
of the lustrous concretion prized as a pearl. This bare, abrupt
description – presented without context or comment – suggests,
I think, both the formation of a poem in the imagination of a

poet and the painful, gradual action of earthly existence upon the human spirit, the slow growth – layer upon layer – of the soul. A conjunction of opposing agencies, the pearl provides an encapsulating image for two over-arching themes in *Lean,* that of the complex interconnections between world and spirit, and the deep reciprocity and complementarity of elemental forces: loss and renewal, motion and rest, condensation and dilution, life and death.

Strange to say, the simplicity of these poems compels the reader to pay close attention to them. The poems consist – in the main – of precise, objective descriptions of objects, places, situations and behaviours. It is for the reader to draw inferences from them, to grasp the implications and resonances latent in the words and images. As if to suggest their thematic pre-occupation with the bare essences of things, the poems are cast in simple, direct syntax, shaped in slender lines and engaged with the concrete and the particular. Between lines and stanzas there are often shifts, gaps and leaps, creating juxtapositions or oblique connections between images. Again, the poet selects and presents phenomena, connections are to be made and conclusions drawn in the mind of the reader.

There is in Slater's poetry something of Taoism, a sense of the flow of the universe, a sense of the interplay and inter-penetration of complementary extremes. In the poem titled "Median," we are presented with the interconnection between

the cacophony created by heavy machinery and workmen
shouting while digging and removing earth and grass and the
quiet in which a lone worker dozes on a porch. Cause and effect
are mutually reflexive. The energy and vitality of the endeavor
in which the sleeping workman participates is subtly contrasted
with his grizzled appearance, a reminder of eventual physical
depletion and mortality. A similar relationship of natural forces
is implied in "Thaw," which treats the destructive effects of
winter freezing upon man-made objects (creating pot holes and
cracks in asphalt, fading painted lines on the pavement) and the
destruction of ice that occurs with the spring thaw.

The theme of reciprocal connection between opposites
occurs again in "Treason" and "Between Displays." In the former
poem, the poet reflects how a swamp in which dead plants and
trees decompose acts as compost for the creation of new life,
even producing lovely and fragrant flowers: "rotten black water
/ distilled as lilies." But Slater declines to leave the reader with
that comfortable but reductive observation, undermining his
own sentiment by adding that the swamp also makes "a good
place to hide a body." Similarly, in "Between Displays," a dead
shark on a beach provides life-saving sustenance for scavengers,
and dawn even while bringing renewal of life to the world also
brings death to still "dozy" Japanese beetles plucked from trees
by arborists. The poem ends with what seems to be an image
suggesting the cyclical to-and-fro, mutually reflexive interaction

of antithetical forces in the world, their reversals and inter-
dependence: "daylong / the ferry chugs / back and / forth across
/ the bay."

Other poems, such as "Hatched," "Sketch," "Intensive
Care," "Observances," and "A Grave Responsibility" focus on
loss of contact, loss of health, loss of life. Yet out of bleak loss,
precious moments are seen to be born, their beauty a con-
sequence of their very fragility and impermanence. The poet is
ever aware of the unhappy nature of much of existence: the
helplessness of fish in a drained pond, the vulnerability of poor
human flesh in a hospital emergency ward, the "low-grade /
boredom or grief" on the faces of passengers in a bus. The world
is a "wound." ("Contact.") But it is also a place of natural beauty
and human meaning. There are mountains and waterfalls,
books and paintings, the delicate colors of pigeons, jasmine and
lotus, conversations by candlelight or in a café over cappuccino,
the "glitter of / moon-lit / snow in the / dark garden." And if
there is death ever present in life, there is life ever present and
everlasting in death. And to help sustain us as we wobble and
flounder through life there is humor to be found in the un-
conscious absurdities of our self-serving contrivances, our wiles
and devices: the incongruous blending of Buddha with Bruce
Lee and neon high rise casinos in modern China; the insensible
self-contradiction of a souvenir shop at Walden Pond offering
$25 t-shirts with a quote from Thoreau reading: *Beware of / any*

enterprise / that requires / new clothes; even a " Burning Bush"
which turns out to be the immolation of an effigy of President
George W. Bush, the barefoot (*à la* Moses) perpetrators of
which have their rapturous political theophany terminated
when they are "doused/ by fire-hose."

In the lean poems of this slim volume, there is much to
admire and much to engage with. Balanced and slant, with
roots and reach, these finely crafted poems confirm John Slater
as a distinctive poetic voice with important things to tell.

Surpassing Pleasure
by John Slater
Erin, Ontario: Porcupine Press
2011

Lean
by John Slate
Niagara Falls, Ontario:
Grey Borders Books
2019

AT THE BORDERS OF BEING
Reading Sally Read

The title of Sally Read's first collection, *The Point of Splitting* is taken from a line in "Confession," one of the poems in the volume: "Before a fruit desiccates / it colours, ripens to the point of splitting." That is the point – both in the natural world and in the realm of human affairs – that holds the poet's the attention and interest in these early poems. That stage, that phase, that exact position or instant, the fulcrum, the fracture, the boundary, the fissure, the rift, the definitive division of then and now, there and here, this and that, ardour and sorrow, life and death. Working as a psychiatric nurse, Read has known much brokenness at close quarters. She has washed and laid out the dead, performed medical tests, administered injections, and given care to demented and dying patients. With the hard-won composure of a combat veteran, these early poems by Read affirm compassion and courage, while encompassing at the same time, passion and sensuality.

Read maintains in her poems a level voice to match her steady eye. Her language is direct, taut, pared down, her words carefully set and joined, but alive with inventions and surprises:

"mute blarney," "stuck delicacy," "clipped acoustics," "blanched seconds," "freeze-bruised," "chilled unsheathing." She savours and celebrates beauty and pleasure – music, art, love – but is ever conscious of their fragility and transience: the imminence, the inevitability of "the point of splitting." Loved ones depart or die, jasmine blossoms and withers, minds are erased by dementia, bodies grow ill, fruits rot, stars fall from the night sky, the tastes of cold beer or margaritas or kisses fade from our tongues. We can prevent nothing, we can only strive to see clearly and to carry on with such integrity and dignity as we can summon. Read offers her readers no easy consolations in these early poems, the cultivation of a stoic (or existential) acceptance is, in the end, the whole point of knowing the point of splitting.

Yet despite their surface poise a deeper urgency at times disturbs certain of Read's early poems, a latent metaphysical yearning – a longing for light. Imagery of light is recurrent: lamplight, sunlight, starlight, moonlight, neon signs, lighted windows, lightning, even lightning bugs. The primal desire for light is most explicit in a poem titled "Winter Light" where a woman gravely stricken with illness craves sunshine and arranges glass objects on a window sill in such a way as to capture and collect the pale light of the winter sun. Her illness and her craving may perhaps be seen to emblematize our common stricken state on this dark earth and our deep-rooted human longing for light, light that might "prize open / the

constricted black whorls of nausea" that sometimes possess us
in our more desolate hours.

Read's second collection, *Broken Sleep,* consists of two
sections: "Broken Sleep" and "The Glass Eye." The first
comprises a sequence of poems giving an account of the
gestation, birth and infancy of the poet's daughter. The process
catalyzes in the mind and spirit of the poet a corresponding
development, suggested already in the opening poem of the
series, "The Crossing," in which enclosed in darkness, deep in
the hull of a ship – like a foetus in a womb – she traverses at
night an expanse of water from one shore and one life to
another shore and a new life there. The title of this section
would seem to have two meanings: a reference to the inter-
rupted sleep experienced by a nursing mother and a naming of
the metamorphosis undergone by the poet-speaker, that is, an
awakening from her former life which now seems to her a kind
of sleep. The awakening is to a new awareness of the world and
to the experience of a new and profound form of love. Even as
the life of the foetus stirs within her, Read feels herself simul-
taneously diminished to the level of a bystander yet raised to a
new, more acute perception of life, including the life of the
natural world. Flowers, fish, birds, fruit, insects, leaves, the
seasonal cycle and the diurnal cycle take on deeper meanings
for her. Sensible of the slow, mysterious, miracle of budding life
within her and later of the tender, precious newborn life in her

care, she begins to enter into a fuller participation in the created world, partly a partaking in and partly a being partaken of. Communication with the unborn and the newly born child takes place at a pre-linguistic, pre-rational level, by means of odors, sounds, rhythms, gazes and touch, re-immersing the poet in the fertile pre-verbal world of infancy: "all words gone." Read finds herself drawn into and being carried along by a current of primal, powerful love, surpassing in depth and strength even that of lovers, a love that is the very measure and purest expression of all human love: the love between child and parent. Such love, Read writes, is "a calling," a summons from and sign of an ultimate Love, that very Love which, as Dante writes, "moves the sun and other stars."

The second section of the volume, titled "The Glass Eye," challenges and complements the tender mood of the first section, presenting imagery of disfigurement, disease, depravity, appalling crime, loss, sorrow, fear and death. Many of the poems in this section make for disturbing reading (as they are, no doubt, intended to do.) Read's newly achieved affirmative and expansive perspective on life as chronicled in the "Broken Sleep" sequence does not cancel her awareness of what is awful and evil in existence. But while acknowledging the raw tragedy of so many lives in the world – murder, matricide, life-blighting maladies and self-destructive obsessions – certain of the poems in this section honor the possibility of heroism and holiness.

There is, for example, a poem titled "On Saint Gianna (1922-62) who died as a result of refusing essential medical treatment in order to save the life of her unborn child," and a poem dedicated to the memory of Anna Mae Pictou-Aquash, an American Indian activist who was brutally murdered by unknown assailants. Another poem, titled "The Baptism," recounts a sudden epiphany experienced by the poet-speaker regarding the deeper implications of Michaelangelo's famed statue, *Pietà*. Encountering the sculpted figures, as if for the first time, the poet "hears" in the speechless, unspeakable suffering of St. Mary holding in her arms her dead son, "not *Look what you have done* / but *"This is what I have."* Human pain, loss and sacrifice may through faith at times be transformed by the sufferers into acts of love suffused with redemptive light. Taking as its subject a happier and more common level of human experience, the final poem of the volume, "Honeymoon in the Midnight Sun," is a celebration of light and love. The longing for light latent in certain of the poems of *The Point of Splitting* has discovered vital sources of sustenance.

An invisible, inviolable light of mind or of spirit informs the poems of Sally Read's third and most recent volume, *The Day Hospital,* sub-titled "A Poem for Twelve Voices." The book is arranged as a sequence of twelve interior monologues taking place in the minds of twelve patients at the Day Hospital (an

outpatient facility) in London's Soho district. The monologues
occur in the course of a single day between the hours of 8 a.m.
and 5 p.m. and are interspersed with evocative, impressionistic
descriptions of the city during those hours: the sights, sounds
and odors of the streets, the light and weathers and the rush of
traffic and commuters travelling to and from urban workplaces.
The individual persons in whose minds the monologues unfold
as silent inner speech are isolated, agéd and damaged, many are
exiles far from home, some traumatized by war. They are Irish,
Polish-Jewish, German-Jewish, Italian-Jewish, Jamaican, Russian
and London-born English. Some are schizophrenic, others
suffer from clinical depression or from Alzheimers, one has
been lobotomized. Each monologue is preceded by a brief
account of the patient, including age and ailment. Their
thoughts and memories are rendered in an unchronological,
fragmented, shifting, associative, stream-of-consciousness style,
pronounced silently within the chambers of their minds in the
dialect of and with the grammar and lexis of the individual.

A common denominator among these pinched and tragic
lives is the presence in each maimed mind of some ineradicable
core of selfhood, some still bright speck or splinter of con-
sciousness that animates them yet, lending to them a hidden
dignity and enabling them to defy or even triumph over their
piteous state. For one patient, preservation of the innermost
essential self expresses itself as a sly, minor act of resistance to

the doctors; for another patient it takes the form of a cherished
memory of childhood and home, while for another it is the
precious memory of a kiss and an erotic encounter; for one
preservation of the residual self takes the form of a physical
compulsion to escape and evade; for another it is expressed as
humour; one finds a curious consolation in the sound of urban
foxes mating in the darkness of the small hours, while another
patient finds transcendence of pain in a determined riding of
her exercise bike; one preserves in relentless rituals of grief the
dear memory of her murdered mother; another finds solace in
words of kindness and mercy spoken to her by the nurses and
therapists; and one despairing, haunted mind can only find
freedom and surcease of sorrow in the act of self-murder.

The city that surrounds these unheard inward voices,
the vast populous city of London in which they endure their
isolated lives, is rendered here as harsh and hectic, clamorous
and malodorous. Beneath the urgent rhythms of the workday
there is a substratum of benumbed futility. Soho promises
piquant diversions in the form of nude shows and "veined, pink
rubber dildos" and crotchless red panties in the windows of sex
shops. Yet there is still a flower stall at the Berwick Street
Market and St. Patrick's Catholic Church on Soho Square still
stands: "Romanesque arches and incense in open darkness."
Grace – however unheeded and disbelieved in – remains
available in natural beauty and in religion. And perhaps that

unseen, silent, beleaguered, precious particle of selfhood to which utterance is given in these twelve monologues may be seen as occupying a "point of splitting" between uniqueness and universality, a point of intersection between the personal and the eternal, a point of convergence with a vaster whole. These poems are, in their several ways, reports from the borders of being.

Sally Read is a poet of many virtues and resources, including a broad tonal range and a firm command of pace and phrasing, a knack for arresting and apposite imagery, keen observation and empathy, clarity of apprehension and depth of meaning. Harrowing and humbling, fierce and lyrical, Read's work offers ample rewards.

The Point of Splitting
by Sally Read
Tarset, U.K. Bloodaxe, 2005

Broken Sleep
by Sally Read
Tarset, U.K. Bloodaxe, 2009

The Day Hospital
by Sally Read
Tarset, U.K. Bloodaxe, 2012

WHAT WILL SUFFICE
The Cistercian Nuns of Tautra Mariakloster

Many of us enjoy reading of lives lived on the edge, that is lives lived dangerously, vividly – soldiers, bullfighters, explorers, spies. Extraordinary, exciting lives. But there are, of course, other kinds of brinks and borders: interior verges, frontiers of the mind and spirit. In this sense (and in other ways, as well) the Cistercian nuns of Mariakloster on the island of Tautra in Norway may be seen to be living lives on the edge, lives devoted to an uncompromising endeavor of growing beyond themselves, lives directed toward a silent inward encounter with Mystery.

The island of Tautra is located in the Trondheims-fjord in the west-central part of Norway, far enough north for the northern lights to be seen in winter. Tautra is a place of seasonal extremes of daylight and darkness, warmth and cold. At the winter solstice, the sun rises at 10:02 a.m. and sets at 2:33 p.m. At the summer solstice, the sun rises at 3: 02 a.m. and sets at 11:37 p.m. while the twilight lingers throughout the brief night. In autumn and winter, storms and gales are not infrequent. Sometimes

snow falls in May. From the year 1207 to 1532, the island
was the site of Tautra Abbey, a Cistercian monastery,
which was dissolved during the reformation and its lands
seized by the crown. (The ruins of the abbey have since
become a popular tourist destination.) The Mariakloster
was established on Tautra in 1999, its foundation stone
laid by Queen Sonja of Norway. The community of
Trappistine nuns (Order of Cistercians of the Strict Ober-
vance) currently occupying the Mariakloster numbers
fourteen, drawn from nine different nationalities. The
sisters support themselves by manufacturing and market-
ing soaps, balms and creams. They also tend a vegetable
garden and a small orchard, grow greenhouse tomatoes,
gather mushrooms and pick and preserve raspberries and
red currants which abound on the island.

 Northern Light consists in the main of accounts by
four nuns resident in the Mariakloster, chronicling the
practices, occupations and events of the year (from New
Year's day to Christmas) as experienced on Tautra. Their
descriptions include carefully observed details of the
island's changing weathers and skies, its flora and its
birdlife. The nuns pursue a rigorous schedule (rising each
morning at 4 a.m.) of prayer, the reading of scripture, the
singing of antiphons, and manual labor. Through most of
the day, they maintain silence among themselves. The

austere simplicity of their lives seems to instill in them a
joyous openness to natural beauty. Wind, waves, stars,
clouds, storms, snowfall, flowers, phases of the moon,
tender spring leaves and many-hued autumn leaves are all
received by them with gratitude and wonder. The sisters
also relish congruences between the turning seasons of the
year and the cycle of liturgical seasons that they observe,
discovering between the two a reciprocal relationship in
which each illuminates the other.

The nuns of Mariakloster live lives on the edge of
society, rejecting consumerism, materialism and the ethos
of instant-gratification in favor of simplicity and a spirit-
ually engaged life. Their inner lives may be said to be lived
on "the razor's edge" (as the *Katha Upanishad* phrases it)
of a personal search for union with God. ("Sharp like a
razor's edge is the path, the sages say, difficult to traverse.")
Their attention is fixed firmly upon essential things and
ultimate concerns, their lives dedicated to an inward
transformation, to a relentless re-shaping and refining of
consciousness, reaching forward beyond the barriers of
self-will and self-centeredness toward self-giving and a
deepening sense of the divine presence.

There is, Mary Shelley wrote, a poetry "which
overflows from the soul." (*Notes to the Complete Poetical
Works of Percy Bysshe Shelly,* 1839.) And there is, as

Wallace Stevens has written, "the poem of the mind in the act of finding / what will suffice." (*Of Modern Poetry.*) Both poetic principles may be seen to be operative in the selection of verses enriching the prose text of *Northern Light* – a dozen or so poems fashioned in free verse and in sonnet form – written by Sister Chen, Sister Berentzen and Sister Bartlett. Their poems reflect disciplined, focused minds deeply embedded in their natural surroundings, deeply connected to the elemental energies of the landscape, and, of course, minds and spirits animated by love of God.

In observing the gradual growth of morning light, the slow, steady lengthening of winter days, Sister Berentzen finds an analogy with the Light redeemed from darkness and with the birth of Christ following hard upon the winter solstice. "July" is a poem of praise to the beautyful, bountiful victory of light at the summit of the solar cycle, and to the way in which – like a fruit-bearing tree – a saint's life can provide to others perennial spiritual refreshment. The flight of bats, the changing colors of aspen leaves, the sound of waves in the fjord: in every season of the turning year, at every hour of the day, Sister Berentzen writes in an untitled poem, we are in receipt of a multitudinous, glorious Divine largesse.

Sister Chen's poems celebrate occasions of grace. In
"Light," she ponders a parallel between the light of distant
stars which having been emitted aeons ago – centuries
before any of us now living existed – reaches our eye in a
present instant of seeing, and God's mysterious grace
which, likewise, sets forth toward us – even before we
need it – to reach us when we most require it. Another
poem (untitled) treats the alertness and discernment
requisite to learning "to touch presence / in emptiness." In
"Integration," a kindly gesture on the part of a priest
breaks the poet-speaker's inward "self-siege," leaving her
"seared, made whole."

Night, dawn, rain, frost, flowers, fruit, tides, clouds,
the barrenness of winter, the bright abundance of summer
– these primary things make up the motifs of Sister
Bartlett's poems. But their deeper theme is that of the
spirit, quickened by the fragile beauty of snowdrops,
finding "calm clarity" in harsh weathers, encountering an
affirmation of redemption even in the winter storm: "From
buffeted night /Christ arises. / In midnight's destitution he
comes / wild and tender / broken and whole." Responding
to the moods and meanings of the natural world, she prays:
"let the vocabulary of creation / ignite the word / inside."

In the end, I wonder, might not all of the Cistercian
sisters living in the Mariakloster be considered as poets of

a kind? Performance poets, if you will, for an audience of
One; collaborating co-authors of a single, sustained,
unfolding poem enacted by them in silence, prayer and
humble labor; poets also by right of having so diligently
sought and found in this world *what will suffice.*

With its handsome color photographs, evocative
poems and rich descriptions of the daily lives of the sisters
through the course of a year – "so ordinary on the surface,
yet extraordinary in the depths" – *Northern Light* will
interest any reader whose concerns or whose curiosity
extend to the psychology of monasticism or contemporary
spirituality. This endearing and worthful book possesses a
quiet capacity to prompt us to reflect seriously upon the
quality of our own lives.

Northern Light:
The Cistercian Nuns of Tautra Mariakloster
by Sr. Cheryl Frances Chen, Sr. Hanne-Maria Berentzen,
Sr. Anne Elizabeth Sweet & Sr. Maria Rafael Bartlett
Athens, Ohio: Cistercian Publications, 2020.